Badlands of the American West:
A Primer

Anthony J. Dzik and Vincent J. Dzik

PLAIN PLATEAU PUBLICATIONS, Portsmouth, Oh

ISBN-13:978-1469954875

ISBN-10:1469954877

DEDICATION

For Justin, our sometimes partner in exploration.

Front cover color photo: Along the Little Missouri River in North Dakota.
Back cover color photo: In the Paint Mines Interpretive Park near Calhan, Colorado.

CONTENTS

ACKNOWLEDGMENTS

First, we thank God for the opportunity to traverse some of the landscapes of His spectacular design. Our sincerest thanks are given to the park rangers and badlands area residents that we met for the stories they told and the directions they gave. Our thanks also go out to several people at Shawnee State University, namely Drs. Dave Todt, Tim Schuerer, Chris Kacir, and Jim Miller, who helped secure some funding for our travel and research. Special thanks to SSU student Thaddeus Bowman for constructing the Medora climograph. Our love and appreciation is given to Drema Dzik for her relentless editing. Special gratitude goes out to Drs. Bill Bloch and Steven Duff of Columbus, Ohio whose good work helped pave the way to our travels.   *—Anthony J. Dzik, January 2012*

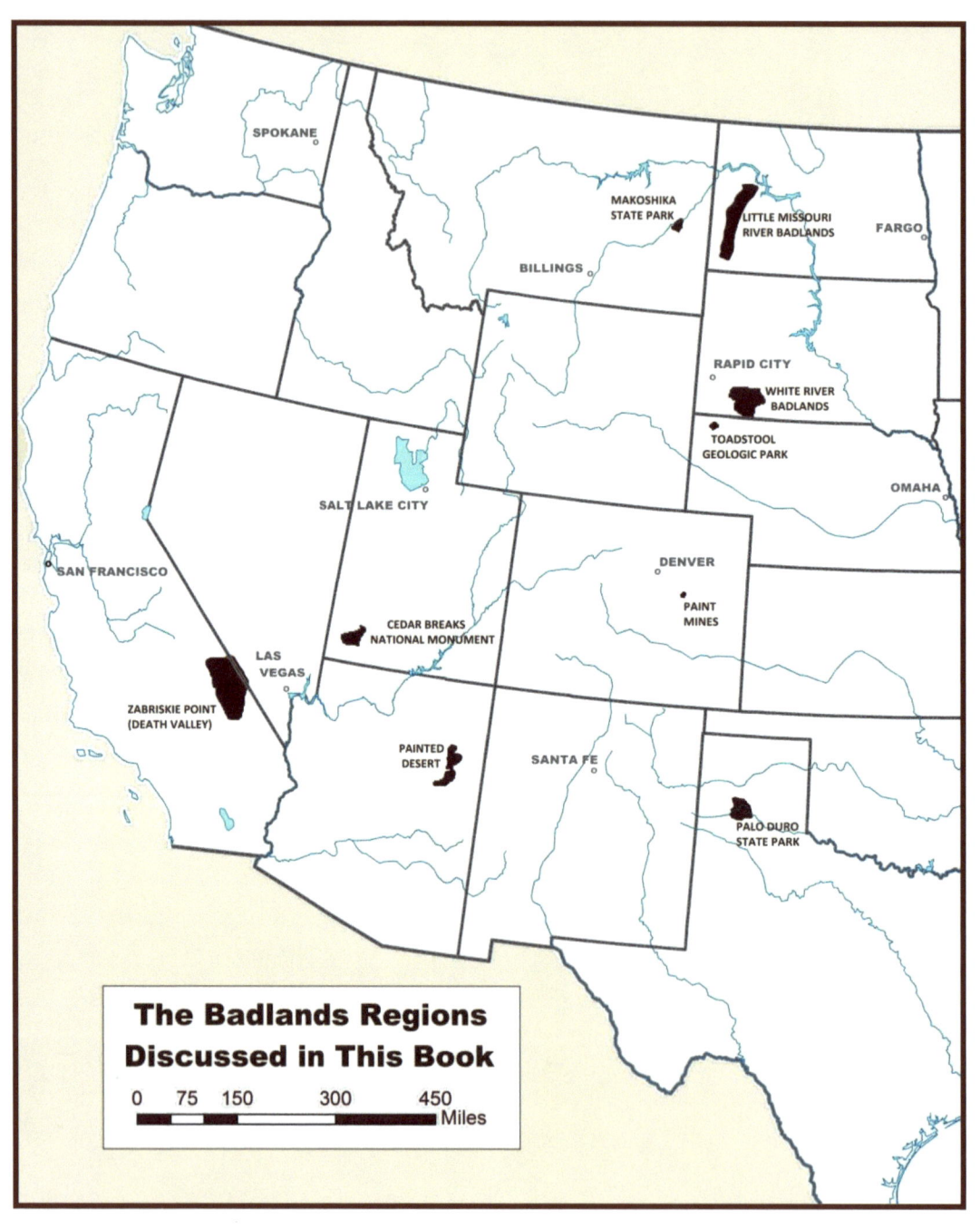

SPOKANE

MAKOSHIKA
STATE PARK

LITTLE MISSOURI
RIVER BADLANDS

FARGO

BILLINGS

RAPID CITY

WHITE RIVER
BADLANDS

TOADSTOOL
GEOLOGIC PARK

OMAHA

SALT LAKE CITY

SAN FRANCISCO

DENVER

PAINT
MINES

CEDAR BREAKS
NATIONAL MONUMENT

LAS
VEGAS

ZABRISKIE POINT
(DEATH VALLEY)

PAINTED
DESERT

SANTA FE

PALO DURO
STATE PARK

The Badlands Regions
Discussed in This Book

0   75   150   300   450
                              Miles

CHAPTER 1.

INTRODUCTION

"Badlands." In some ways, that is a terrible word used to describe some of the dry dissected sedimentary landscapes of the western Great Plains and American Southwest. French fur trappers called the rugged country along South Dakota's White River and along North Dakota's Little Missouri *"les mauvaises terres a traverse"*, "bad lands to traverse." The Sioux before them called such terrain *"maco sica"* meaning land of bad spirits or "badlands". Yet, members of both cultures were intrigued by the combination of stunning beauty and abject desolation that they encountered around every butte, gully, and slide in this rough landscape. So, yes, it may have been bad to cross, but it was marvelous to view.

Sunlight and storm accentuate the stark grandeur of the badlands environment. The colors of the rock and **regolith** seem to change with the daily and seasonal changes in the sun's path in the sky. Cloudbursts temporarily alter the natural palette and reconfigure the rock formations. Badlands are landscapes that are ever-changing in ways great and small.

Over the course of several years, we journeyed through a number of badlands regions in the United States. We drove the official scenic routes as well as unpaved rural roads and we hiked the marked trails and the backcountry. Our purpose was to compare and contrast the badlands of different places in order to prepare a modest book describing various badlands features in plain language. All photographs were taken by the authors.

Figure 1. Just outside of Glendive, Montana is an almost surreal 11,400-acre preserve called Makoshika State Park. These are the badlands of the Yellowstone River and its tributaries. Like all badlands landscapes, Makoshika exhibits an assortment of sawtooth ridges, fluted mesas, remnant buttes, pinnacles, hoodoos, gullied slopes, rain pillars, and caprocks which bedeck the land with color.

CHAPTER 2.

THE PHYSICAL GEOGRAPHY OF BADLANDS

Badlands are a landscape that resembles a miniature mountain range carved in weak sedimentary rocks, particularly shales and clays, by running water and wind in arid and semi-arid climates. In the United States, badlands occur on the western Great Plains in the Dakotas, Montana, Nebraska, Colorado, and Texas. Other badlands are part of the arid basin-and-plateau country of New Mexico, Nevada, Utah, Arizona, and California. In these parched environments where vegetation tends to be sparse, erosion by running water is very effective in sculpting and removing sedimentary earth materials. Sedimentary rock is formed from the deposition/accumulation and eventual lithification (hardening) of loose mineral (and sometimes organic) sediments laid down by water, wind, or glacial ice. With regard to badlands, the sediments are largely water- and wind-deposited.

Although badlands may bear a resemblance to a mountain range, the way they develop and the way we encounter them is totally different. Mountains loom up from the horizon and are easily seen from a distance, but one must look down to see badlands. The Hispanos of New Mexico used to say *"Hay las sierras debajo de los llanos"* which basically translates to "There are mountains below the plains" (Figure 2). In some cases, such as at Cedar Breaks National Monument (Figure 3) in southwestern Utah, one might say "there are mountains below the mountains."

Figure 2. Looking down from the Llano Estacado upon the badlands on the floor of Palo Duro Canyon. Clearly seen in the buttes are several formations. The reddish Quartermaster ends and the yellowish, gray, and lavender mudstones, shales, and sandstones of the Tecovas begin. The Tecovas and the Quartermaster combined form the triangular layers of the Spanish Skirts. The colorful Spanish Skirts occur on steep slopes that are devoid of vegetation and exhibit rill erosion. The white stripes are typically layers of satin spar gypsum.

Figure 3. On the edge of the Colorado Plateau in Utah is the Cedar Breaks National Monument. Shaped like a huge coliseum, the amphitheater is more than 2000 feet deep and more than 3 miles in diameter. All the hoodoos, arches, fins, and draws have been carved by running water, carbonic acid action, wind, and frost action. Cedar refers to the juniper trees that early settlers mistook for cedars. Breaks is an older term for badlands.

Figure 4. The White River Badlands in South Dakota are perhaps the world's best known badlands region.

Badlands slopes tend to have sparse vegetation that contributes to high rates of erosion. Water and wind, instead of carving gentle hills and broad valleys, sculpt the softer sedimentary rocks into intricate mazes of narrow ravines, v-shaped gullies, knife-sharp ridges, buttes, and colorful pinnacles. For badlands to form, the land must be composed of alternating layers of hard and soft rocks, regolith, and soil. When easily eroded material, such as clay or mud stone, is topped by more resistant material, such as sandstone, the harder horizontal layers offer some protection to the beds of soft deposits below. Uncovered layers of softer rocks or soil wash away quickly, while protected deposits form nearly vertical walls beneath the harder material.

The primary agent of erosion is usually water. Rain in the semiarid badlands often falls in sudden, heavy showers. The water moves swiftly, washing down the exposed hills, loosening grains and particles of rock. Deep gullies and channels are the result.

Figure 5. Deep gully at Palo Duro State Park in the Texas Panhandle.

Shale-derived badland surface soils are subject to gravitational down-slope movement, especially after a rainstorm.   The loose colluvium, especially if over shale bedrock, is likely to result in landslides and slumping (Figure 6).

Figure 6. Slump block in the North Unit of Theodore Roosevelt National Park near Watford City, North Dakota. The slump block has slipped down the hill at least 150 feet. Compare the tilted orientation of the bedding in the slump block relative to the horizontal bedding in the butte in the background. Slumping like this is the result of undercutting and occurs where canyon or butte sides are too weak to support a top heavy formation.

As indicated before, the climates of badlands regions in the United States are dry (semi-arid to arid). The most significant difference between regional climates is temperature. The badlands areas in the northern Great Plains have a variable and unpredictable climate. The climograph (Figure 7) for Medora, North Dakota illustrates the Dry Midlatitude Steppe climate (Koppen classification BSk) typical of the Little Missouri River Badlands. Most badlands regions of the northern Plains receive less than 18 inches of precipitation annually. The summers are hot and dry with occasional violent thunderstorms. Winters are typically cold with 12 to 24 inches of total snowfall. Extremely high winds are common year-round. Sudden and dramatic weather changes are common. Summer daytime skies are usually clear. The badlands of the Great Plains generally support steppe-like grassland. Taller western wheatgrass, green needlegrass, and needle-and-thread grass dominate low moist spots while shortgrass communities of blue grama and buffalo grass cover drier, rocky outcrops. Knolls and less-steep breaks frequently show development of pine savanna-type cover with scattered Ponderosa pine (*Pinus ponderosa*) or Rocky Mountain juniper-pine associations. **Xerophytes** (plants adapted to a dry environment) such as prickly pear cacti can be found here and there.

Because of latitude, the climate of the badlands of the southern Plains is noticeably warmer. The mean annual temperature for Palo Duro Canyon in Texas is about 59°F. The Paint Mines in eastern Colorado are a special case as they are situated on the western edge of the Plains in the shadow of the Front Range of the Rockies and the average elevation of 6670 feet above sea level is noticeably higher than that of other High Plains badlands. Because of the high elevation, summer monthly mean temperatures are less than 70° F and the January mean is 24° F. During summer in particular there is a large diurnal temperature range because of the generally clear skies. Summer daytime temperatures can be quite warm but nighttime temperatures can drop into the fifties because of radiational cooling. As the area is in the **rainshadow** of the Rockies, annual precipitation is low (14.9

inches) and the winter months tend to be dry. The composition of the soft clay also has an effect on the rate of erosion. Badlands clay soaks up precipitation somewhat like a sponge. As it dries, the exposed soil cracks and crumbles, leaving loose regolith several inches deep on the surface of the ground. This detritus begins to wash away immediately, often during the next severe storm. Lack of dense vegetative ground cover makes erosion easier.

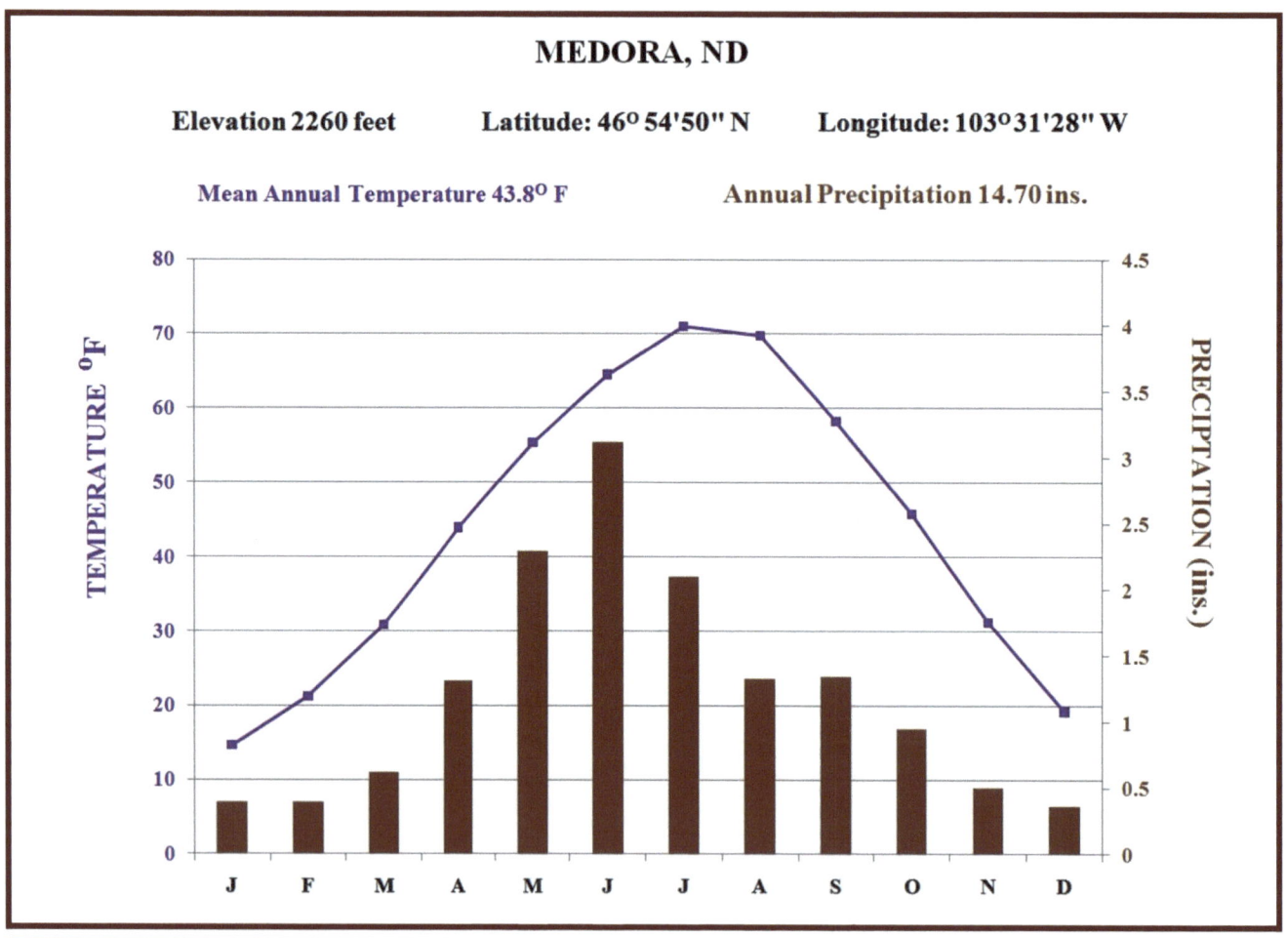

Figure 7. Climograph for Medora, North Dakota illustrates the BSk climate of northern Great Plains badlands area. *(Climograph constructed by T. Bowman)*

Figure 8. Typical northern plains vegetation in the area around Magpie Creek in North Dakota's Little Missouri River Badlands.

In the Paint Mines, the open plains are covered by a mix of short-grass and mid-grass **prairie** dominated by blue grama and buffalo grass. Watercourses in the area tend to flow intermittently and many are dry over much of the year (Figure 9). Where there is sufficient water in the stream bottoms, the vegetation is more varied with diverse grasses, low sagebrush, chokecherry, sedges, and random short-stature pines and junipers.

Figure 9. Dry steam bed in the Paint Mines Badlands near Calhan, Colorado.

A much drier climate reigns over the desert badlands of the basin-and-plateau country of the American Southwest. The Painted Desert in Arizona receives about 10 inches of precipitation annually and the Zabriskie Point Badlands of California's Death Valley will be fortunate if they see a little over 2 inches of rainfall in a year. These are true desert climates and Death Valley is hot and average daily maximums in the summer months commonly exceed 100 °F. As a consequence, vegetation is practically lacking at Zabriskie Point (Figure 10).

Figure 10. Badlands at Zabriskie Point in Death Valley. Vegetation is not to be seen.

Badlands are characterized by rugged relief. Figure 11 shows a portion of the USGS Medora, North Dakota quadrangle. The contour lines are very close together indicating dramatic changes in elevation. While canyons are generally formed along the main channel of a river, the development of badlands topography extends back toward the headwaters of the numerous creeks that drain into the main stream. In some areas these creeks are so close together that the badlands of one overlap those of the next, creating a labyrinth of cliffs, ravines, gullies, and gorges. Over most of the Little Missouri River Badlands region, maximum relief is in the range of 200 to almost 500 feet. Locally, some of the steep slopes are conducive to excessive runoff, and deep wide ditches and gullies pass through most of the "feeder" creek valleys.

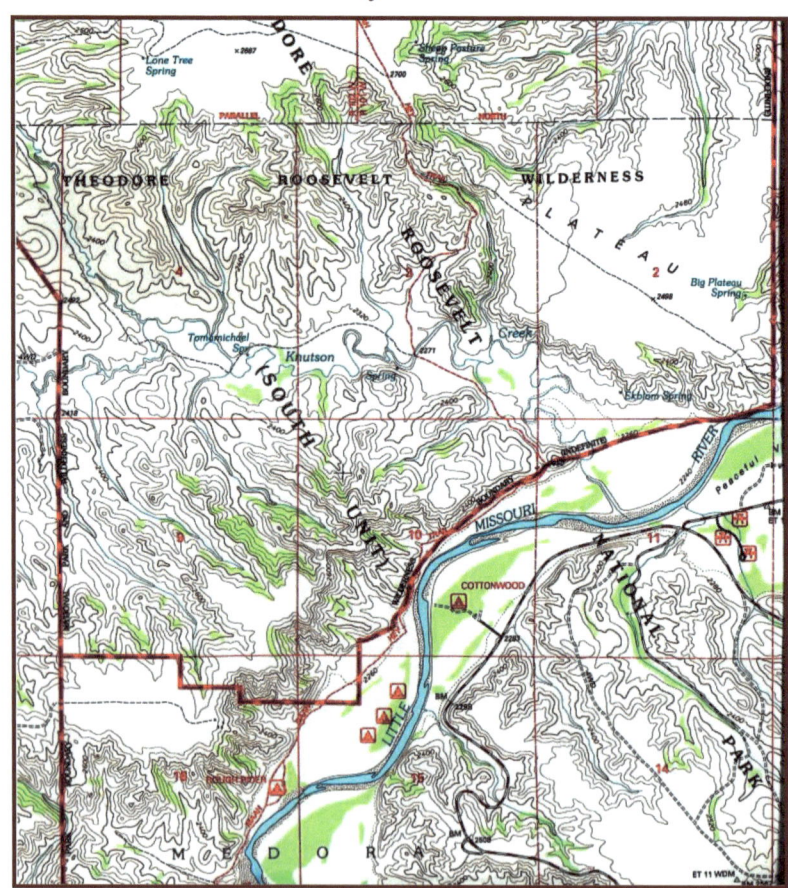

Figure 11. 1:24000 topographic map of a portion of the South Unit of Theodore Roosevelt National Park in southwestern North Dakota. The rugged relief of badlands is clearly seen in the close spacing of contour lines. Elevations on the floodplain of the Little Missouri River are about 2240 feet asl while many of the butte summits top 2500 feet. Also note the maze of numerous intermittent stream channels.

CHAPTER 3.

THE GEOLOGY AND DEVELOPMENT OF BADLANDS

Most badlands in the American West share some aspects of geologic history and development, but there are also some differences between regions. The geologic history of the badlands of the western Great Plains is tied mainly to events beginning with the Laramide **Orogeny** (the birth of the Rocky Mountains) which occurred about 65 or so million years ago. We first present the stories of North Dakota's Little Missouri River Badlands and that of White River Badlands of South Dakota and Nebraska.

The sediments that became the horizontal sedimentary rock strata visible in the Little Missouri River Badlands were deposited on a swampy plain between 55 and 65 million years ago by streams flowing from the rising Rocky Mountains to the west. The badlands topography began forming approximately 600,000 years ago when an advancing continental glacier diverted the north-flowing Little Missouri River to the east at a point near the North Unit of Theodore Roosevelt National Park. The river then ran faster and cut quickly down through the layers of soft sedimentary rock as it flowed down this shorter, steeper path. Since that time, the river and its tributaries have been carving an exceptionally rugged landscape. The Little Missouri River itself is dynamic. It meanders within its banks and changes its course over time. It flows fast with spring run-off and slows to a trickle during most summers. Erosion by running water and wind along with physical weathering and **mass wasting** continuously are at work reconfiguring the landscape.

The sediments in the region largely belong to the Fort Union Group which is divided into three formations (rock units defined by different compositional traits) of which two, the Bullion Creek and Sentinel Butte formations, are seen throughout much of the badlands. The third and oldest formation, the Cannonball, represents the actual transition from aquatic to terrestrial deposition and is deeply buried. The Bullion Creek and Sentinel Butte formations are rather similar and are composed of stratified yellowish-gray and olive-gray sand, silt, and clay, together with numerous veins of **lignite** (Figure 12). Reddish bands of clinker, locally called scoria (Figure 13), add color to the rocks. The Bullion Creek formation is rather beige and the overlying Sentinel Butte tends to be greyer. The upper layers of these formations are composed of sandstone and shale.

Around 70 million years ago is the beginning of the South Dakota Badlands story. At that time the area was part of a shallow inland sea (sometimes called the Pierre Sea) in which were deposited fine sediments washed down from higher land in the west. Then came the Laramide Orogeny which built up the Rocky Mountains causing the Pierre Sea to drain away by the Eocene Epoch 37-55 million years ago. Erosion of the Pierre shale created a rolling hilly landscape and the exposed seabed changed in color from grey to yellow.

Near the end of the Eocene (37 million years ago), sediments washed down from the ancestral Black Hills and streams filled an ancient valley, overflowed their banks and deposited lots of sediment across the landscape. These sediments are evidenced today by thin grey clays of the Chadron formation. The most steeply eroded scenery in the White River Badlands is carved from the accumulations of sediments laid down during the Oligocene Epoch (26 to 34 million years ago). Over 400 feet of sand, silt, and clay overlies the Chadron Formation and is called the Brule Formation. The Brule Formation also contains some ash layers deposited from volcanic eruptions in the Rocky Mountains.

Figure 12. A vein of lignite coal exposed in the Little Missouri River Badlands of North Dakota. The lignite is formed from vegetation that died and was buried in the Paleocene swamps. The partially decomposed vegetation (peat) was covered by layers of silt and clay deposited by rivers. In time the weight of the overlying sediments led to lithification and carbonation of the organic matter.

Figure 13. Lightning strikes and prairie fires can ignite veins of lignite coal which can burn for many years. As the lignite burns, it bakes the overlying sediments into a hard, natural brick locally called "scoria." The red color comes from the oxidation of iron released from the coal as it burns. Scoria is more resistant to erosion than the unbaked Tertiary strata nearby. Over time, erosion wears down the less resistant rocks, leaving behind knobs, ridges, and buttes topped with red scoria caps.

Figure 14. Toadstool Geologic Park near Crawford, Nebraska. This area along Big Cottonwood Creek is related to the White River Badlands of South Dakota. The oldest exposed rocks here are of the Chadron Formation, layers of fine-grained, light-brown and pinkish claystones formed mainly from volcanic ash. Overlying the Chadron is the Brule Formation. The Brule is composed of a variety of sedimentary rocks such as siltstones, a few tuffaceous layers (volcanic ash beds), claystones, and sandstones rich in quartz and feldspar. The Chadron and Brule make up the White River Group.

The development of the badlands at Zabriskie Point in Death Valley begins with the deposition of fine-grained sediments in a prehistoric lake that existed some nine million years ago. These sediments were silts, muds, and gravels from the erosion of nearby mountains and ashfalls from the Black Mountain volcanic field (eruptions about five million years ago). Together these materials formed the Furnace Creek Formation. Iron oxides add color (mostly yellows and browns) to the rocks and volcanic ash provides the gray and greenish tints. Orogeny to the west produced a drier climate, causing the lake to dry up. The subsequent widening and sinking of Death Valley and another uplift of the Black Mountains tilted the region. Then the relentless erosional work of running and wind began to dissect the sedimentary layers and create the badlands. Rainfall at Zabriskie Point doesn't occur very often, but when it does, it is in the form of an intense downpour. With hardly any vegetation and little soil cover, there is little infiltration. Runoff in such an environment is spectacular, creating numerous **rills** in the soft rock of the Furnace Creek formation. Over time the rills cut deeper to form gullies and a labyrinth of various sized channels develops.

Figure 15. Zabriskie Point in Death Valley National Park.

The geologic story of the badlands of Arizona's Painted Desert is partly the story of the Four Corners region of the Colorado Plateau. The Colorado Plateau is a high standing crustal block of horizontal sedimentary strata. Many of the sedimentary rocks exposed on the Colorado Plateau were deposited at or near sea level 240 to 65 million years ago. About 5 million years ago the entire Rocky Mountains and Colorado Plateau were uplifted 4,000 to 6,000 feet. On the Colorado Plateau, the uplift was accompanied by a tilting of the plateau toward the north. Rivers like the Colorado and Green established their courses at this time and because they were lifted high above base level they began to downcut dramatically and entrench their channels. Differential erosion of the plateau thus began and various badlands developed in this semi-arid to arid tableland.

The Painted Desert is characterized by stratified layers of weak siltstone, mudstone, and shale of the Triassic Chinle Formation. Most of these sediments were lain down by streams flowing northwestwardly out of Utah and across northern Arizona. When exposed to the agents of denudation for even a short time the Chinle formation usually develops a badlands topography. Resistant sandstones and conglomerates tend to form cliffs and cap the flat-topped mesas. Softer shales and mudstones erode faster and usually form more conical hills and mounds. The rock layers abound with iron and manganese compounds that provide the pigments for the various colors of the region. When sediments are deposited slowly, oxides of iron and aluminum become concentrated in the soil. These concentrations create the red, orange, and pink colors that are quite prominent in the region. During a rapid sediment buildup, oxygen gets removed from the soil and this forms the blue, gray, and lavender layers. Thin resistant lacustrine (from lakes) limestone layers and basaltic lava flows cap some of the mesas. A number of layers of volcanic ash occur in the Chinle Formation and provide the silica for the petrified forests of the area (Part of the Painted Desert lies within Petrified Forest National Park).

Figure 16. The occasional convectional summer thunderstorm over the Painted Desert Badlands accentuates the colors and intensifies erosion.

In Colorado, the Denver Basin was created when the Laramide Front Range developed about 60 million years ago. As the mountains were growing upward, a large basin developed next to them. Over time, the basin filled with layer after layer of sediments eroded from the recently formed mountains. There is some dispute as to the geologic origin of the Paint Mines Badlands of the Denver Basin near Calhan, Colorado. Some geologists identify the badlands as developing upon an alluvial fan projection from the early Rocky Mountains while others contend they may have formed upon a lake deposit. What is agreed is that the Paint Mines are formed from the Dawson Arkose, a sedimentary rock formation laid down about 55 million years ago. Dawson Arkose is composed mainly of thick beds of conglomerates and sandstones rich in feldspar and thin mudstone beds containing plant fossils (petrified hardwoods) and even some veins of lignite coal.

Native Americans who lived here before Euro-American encroachment used the colorful clays to make pottery and ceremonial paint. Later, in the early 1900s, Euro-American settlers mined the clay to manufacture bricks. In fact some buildings in downtown Denver were constructed of brick made from these clays. Once on private land, but preserved since 2006 as the 750-acre Paint Mines Interpretive Park by the El Paso County Parks and Leisure Services system, these badlands could be the most colorful ones on the Plains region (Figure 17). The fanciful colors occur because the clays, like those in Arizona's Painted Desert, are laced with iron oxide.

The badlands at Cedar Breaks National Monument in southwestern Utah are somewhat unusual because of the high elevation at which they sit. They are located on the Markagunt Plateau (a section of the Colorado Plateau) and the rim of the natural amphitheatre containing the badlands is slightly above 10,000 feet asl. A little over sixty-million years ago this area was at the bottom of a seventy mile long lake. Over time, sedimentary deposits filled the ancient lake. Uplift of the region followed. The sediments eventually changed from loose strata to hard strata. Iron, oxygen and water combined, giving the coral color to the sediments. These sediments became the siltstone, sandstone and limestone of the Claron formation of Cedar Breaks.

Figure 17. The colorful Paint Mines Badlands of eastern Colorado. With the right lighting conditions, they can resemble a melting half-eaten ice cream sundae.

Figure 18. Cedar Breaks in Utah. Alpine meadow vegetation is found in some places on the rim as elevations there exceed 10,000 feet.

CHAPTER 4.

COMMON BADLANDS LANDFORMS

There are many magnificent erosional landforms large and small to be encountered in the badlands regions of the American West. Most result from the fact that the various sedimentary rock strata possess different degrees of resistance to the agents of denudation. For the most part, sandstones resist erosion better than do softer rocks such as claystones and shales. Limestone is a bit tricky to categorize because it is susceptible to weathering by carbonic acid action and in wet climates gets reduced quite easily, but in dry climates it is a bit more resistant and may stand higher on the landscape.

The large landform that dominates the badlands is the **butte** (Figure 19). Buttes are the remnants of mesas. A **mesa** is a flat-topped hill usually capped by a resistant rock layer. Mesas develop from the dissection of the horizontal sedimentary strata of a plateau or elevated plains surface. In differentiating mesas and buttes, some geographers would say that a mesa has a top wider than its height while a butte's top is smaller than its height. Over time, running water and wind work to totally consume the buttes (Figure 20).

Very common in badlands are small landforms called **hoodoos**. In most badlands, hoodoos range in height from few feet to over 60 feet high. Hoodoos are irregularly shaped sedimentary rock features that resemble misshapen pillars, spires, columns, and other weird projections. Hoodoos are also known as tent rocks, fairy chimneys, pedestal rocks,

Figure 19. Scoria-capped buttes dominate the landscape at the Painted Canyon Overlook in Theodore Roosevelt National Park near Medora, North Dakota.

Figure 20. Butte remnant south of Badlands National Park, South Dakota. The caprock is limestone. On average, the White River Badlands of South Dakota erode one inch per year.

mushroom rocks, dells, and earth pillars. The primary difference between hoodoos and pinnacles (spires) is that hoodoos have a variable thickness while pinnacles or spires tend to have a smoother profile that widens from the tip down to the ground. Hoodoos develop through differential weathering and erosion controlled by variations in rock resistance and by internal structure or **joints**. Layers of rock with different degrees of resistance to erosion, and with a variety of joint patterns, can be fashioned into very weird and wonderful shapes by the erosional action of water and wind and by mechanical weathering, particularly frost action and salt crystal growth. Hoodoos can develop in all kinds of rock and in semi consolidated sediments; they are most common in sandstone, clay, siltstone, salt deposits, and some carbonate rocks (Figures 21and 22).

Figure 21. Typical hoodoos in Colorado's Paint Mines formed when a resistant cap of white sandstone shielded a column of weak clay below. The pillar formed as materials surrounding the cap rock were eroded by runoff. Hoodoos tend to be found bordering steep slopes and are the last vestiges of the slope as it erodes back. A hoodoo may occur as an isolated bizarre "tower", but they usually occur in groups during the dissection of a plateau surface.

Figure 22. Hoodoos in Makoshika State Park near Glendive, Montana.

Another fascinating feature in areas of badlands is the rain pillar or "toadstool" (Figure 23). The toadstools are comprised of resistant sandstone blocks balanced upon columns of softer clay and siltstone. The sandstone forms a protective cap over the stem of the weaker sedimentary rock below, forming a "toadstool." As the softer clay and siltstone continue to be consumed through erosion, the cap will begin to lean and eventually may slide off its pedestal.

Figure 23. The toadstools which lend their name to Toadstool Geologic Park in the badlands along Big Cottonwood Creek (a tributary of the White River) in the Nebraska panhandle.

The arrangement and shapes of badlands landforms are affected in part by the presence of hard resistant nodules and **concretions** embedded within more easily eroded sedimentary materials. Some concretions and nodules are spherical and are commonly called cannonballs. Round concretions like those weathering out of the cliff in Figure 24 are formed by the cementing action of groundwater.   For millions of years groundwater seeped through the sediments that make up the sandstone layer from an ancient river deposit. The concretions formed by the selective precipitation from ground water of dissolved minerals, most commonly calcium carbonate. As these minerals precipitated, they filled in pore spaces between grains of sand and cemented them together. Cannonballs can be two to three feet in diameter. They may contain a small nucleus of organic material (a shell or plant fragment).

Figure 24. Concretions. These round masses have been emerging from the side of Battleship Butte in the North Unit of Theodore Roosevelt National Park in North Dakota.

CHAPTER 5.

IMAGES OF LIFE PAST AND PRESENT

Many people would think that these stark rugged dry environments would not be hospitable for many life forms. The reality is that the badlands regions are inhabited by a rich variety of flora and fauna. They also contain fossil records of living things from past climatic environments. In the pages that follow we provide a sampling of badlands flora and fauna of the past and present.

Figure 25. Feral horses graze in the South Unit of Theodore Roosevelt National Park. These equines are descendents of runaways from the late 1800s.

Figure 26. Great herds of bison once roamed the Great Plains until their numbers were decimated by wanton wasteful hunting. In recent decades small herds have been reintroduced into several badlands areas. This bull calls the South Unit of Theodore Roosevelt National Park his home.

Figure 27. Bighorn sheep once deftly negotiated the craggy slopes and draws of many badlands areas. Sadly, they were hunted to near extinction. Today, some have been reintroduced into places such as Badlands National Park in South Dakota.

Figure 28. A very common deer in the lands west of the Missouri River is the mule deer, called such because of its large mule-like ears. They are regularly seen throughout the badlands of the northern Great Plains.

Figure 29. In the badlands about fifteen miles northeast of Amidon, North Dakota, is a rather unique stand of Rocky Mountains Junipers. These trees are termed "columnar junipers" and their tapered shape is believed to have developed because of gases emitted by a burning vein of lignite. The burning vein that affected these trees smoldered from about 1880 until the 1970s. After the fire died out, some of the trees reverted to their typical globular bush-like shape.

Figure 30. Prickly Pear cacti and mesquite are common plants on the floor of Palo Duro Canyon south of Amarillo, Texas.

Figures 31 and 32. Prairie dog "towns" can be found in some Great Plains badlands. Prairie dog colonies help support the biodiversity of the Great Plains by attracting a variety of animal species. Bison, for example, are attracted to the colonies to graze on nutrient-rich grasses. Prairie dogs excavate large amounts of soil to the surface and bison like to roll in the dust to rid themselves of parasites. In the hours around dusk, coyotes may visit these communities in search of supper. Both scenes are from the South Unit of Theodore Roosevelt National Park.

HYRACODON ("running rhino") tracks in a rock slab of the Brule formation in Nebraska

Figure 33. While the Nebraska panhandle is semi-arid today, the climate 30 million years ago was humid subtropical. Rhinoceroses, camels, and "Hell pigs" walked the region. Toadstool has given up numerous fossils and has the longest known vertebrate trackway in the world.

Figure 34. Portion of *Poebrotherium* camel jaw and teeth. This fossil was found on a ranch in the White River Badlands near the Nebraska-South Dakota border. It is from the Oligocene Epoch (about 38 million years ago. *Poebrotherium* was a small (3 ½ foot high) camel with a llama-like head and no hump. It's a little-known fact that the first camels evolved in North America and that these pioneering cud-chewing mammals only later spread to North Africa and the Middle East, where most modern camels are found today.

Figure 35. The Petrified Forest in the Wilderness area of the South Unit of Theodore Roosevelt National Park is the 3rd largest petrified wood area in the U.S. During the Paleocene epoch, between 67 and 55 million years ago, western North Dakota was home to subtropical forests with bald cypress, magnolias, and palm trees, some 100 feet tall. These forests were buried by flooding and volcanic ash. Groundwater moving through the silica-rich sediments and volcanic ash dissolved the silica. Silica-rich water then soaked into the buried trees, dissolved the organic compounds and replaced them with small crystals of quartz. A lot of the internal structure of the trees was preserved in this process. The petrified wood occurs as entire logs, stumps, and as scattered limbs and fragments providing us with evidence the climate of a different time.

GLOSSARY

ALLUVIUM—Unconsolidated sediments (sand, silt, gravel, or clay) deposited by streams.

BREAKS—Deeply dissected country usually near streams. Can also refer to badlands.

BUTTE—Steep-sided hill often capped by a resistant rock layer. Buttes are usually mesa remnants.

CAPROCK—Strata of erosion-resistant sedimentary rock, usually limestone, which forms the top layer of mesas and buttes.

CONGLOMERATE—A sedimentary rock composed of durable rounded pebbles and cobbles cemented within a matrix of sand.

CONCRETION—A hard often rounded mineral mass that forms in sediments before they lithify. Chemical changes cause minerals to come out of the groundwater and cement the sediment together.

DENUDATION—The overall lowering of the land surface by weathering, erosion, and sediment transportation.

HOODOO—Any irregularly shaped sedimentary feature in a badlands environment that resembles a misshapen pillar or spire.

INTERMITTENT .STREAM—A stream that flows after a rainfall, but then dries up until the next precipitation event.

JOINTS—Natural fractures in rock. In sedimentary rock, they are usually the result of differential compaction or faulting.

LIGNITE—A brownish-black, soft coal that has about 70 percent carbon content, low BTU value, and a high moisture content.

LITHIFY—Change from a layer of loose sediments to hard strata.

MASS WASTING—Spontaneous downward movement of soil, rock, and regolith.

MESA—Small table-topped plateau bordered on all sides by cliffs and capped by a resistant sedimentary rock layer or lava flow.

OROGENY—A time of mountain-building. The Rocky Mountains formed during the Laramide Orogeny about 65 million years ago.

PRAIRIE—An expanse of nearly level to undulating grassland.

RAINSHADOW—A dry zone on the leeward side (away from the wind) of a mountain range.

REGOLITH—Weathered rock debris found on the land surface.

RELIEF—The range of topographic variation within a given area usually measured in differences in elevation.

RILL EROSION—A type of accelerated erosion characterized by numerous tiny channels incised into bare slopes.

SEDIMENTARY ROCK— Rock that forms from sediments that have accumulated on dry land or in water. Some of these rocks like sandstone and shale represent accumulations of broken-up particles of other rocks that have been transported by water, wind, or glacial ice. Others like limestone are formed from mineral compounds deposited from salt solutions of seawater or saline inland lakes.

STRATUM—Layer of sedimentary rock that generally has the same sediment throughout and normally has other recognizably different layers (strata) above and below it.

TUFFACEOUS—Containing volcanic ash.

XEROPHYTE—A plant adapted to a dry environment. Cacti are xerophytes.

SELECTED REFERENCES

Bluemle, J. P.   1983: Geology of Billings, Golden Valley, and Slope Counties. North Dakota Geological Survey Bulletin No. 76.

Boye, Alan   2007: **The Complete Roadside Guide to Nebraska.** University of Nebraska Press, Lincoln, NE.

Breed, W.J. and C.S. Breed (eds.)   1972: Investigations in the Triassic Chinle Formation. Museum of Northern Arizona Bulletin # 47, Flagstaff, AZ.

Casey, Kidron   2001: **Borderlands of the Sky: Western North Dakota.** Sideroads LLC, Takoma Park, MD.

Dzik, Anthony J.   1978: Compage of Billings County, North Dakota: Economic Activities in a Badlands Environment. Unpublished Master's thesis, Dept. of Geography, University of Toledo.

Flores, Dan   2010: **Caprock Canyonlands.** Texas A & M University Press, College Station, TX.

Froiland, Sven G.   1990: **Natural History of the Black Hills and Badlands**. Center For Western Studies, Sioux Falls, SD.

Gildart, Bert and Jane Gildart 2005: **Death Valley National Park: A Guide to Exploring the Great Outdoors.** Morris Book Publishing. Gilford, CT.

Hogan, Eric.   2001: **The Geography of South Dakota.** Center for Western Studies, Sioux Falls, SD.

Houk, Rose   1990: **The Painted Desert: Land of Light and Shadow.** Petrified Forest Museum Association.

Johnsgaard, Paul A.   2001: **The Nature of Nebraska: Ecology and Biodiversity.** University of Nebraska Press, Lincoln, NE.

Kaye, Bruce M. and Henry A. Schoch 1999: **Theodore Roosevelt National Park: The Story Behind the Scenery.** KC Publications, Las Vegas, NV

Leach, Nicky   1994: **Cedar Breaks National Monument.** Zion Natural History Association, Springfield, UT.

Martin, James E. 1985. Fossiliferous Cenozoic deposits of western South Dakota and northwestern Nebraska. *Dakoterra* 2 2(7), South Dakota School of Mines and Technology. Rapid City, SD.

Miller, Marli B. and Lauren A. Wright   2004: **Geology of Death Valley National Park.** Kendall Hunt, Dubuque, IA.

Murphy, Edward C., J.W. Hoganson, and N. F. Forsman   1993: The Chadron, Brule, and Arikaree Formations in North Dakota-- The Buttes of Southwestern North Dakota. North Dakota Geological Survey Report of Investigation No. 96.

O'Hara, C.C.   1920: The White River Badlands. South Dakota School of Mines Bulletin # 13, Rapid City, SD.

Stokes, Wiliiam Lee   1969: **Scenes of the Plateau Lands and How They Came to Be**. Starstone Publishing, Salt Lake City, UT.

Trimble, Donald E.   1980: **The Geologic Story of the Great Plains.** United States Geological Survey Bulletin 1493.

Wright, Jack 2000: **Montana Places: Exploring Big Sky Country**. University Minnesota Press, Minneapolis, MN.

ABOUT THE AUTHORS

Vincent J. Dzik *(left)* holds the Associate of Individualized Studies degree from Shawnee State University (2011) and is continuing his studies toward a B.I.S. with concentrations in Business Applications and Geo-studies. He hopes to someday work for the National Park Service.

Anthony J. Dzik *(right)* holds the Ph.D. in Geography from Northwestern Univeristy (1986). He is Professor of Geography at Shawnee State University in Portsmouth, Ohio. His teaching and research interests are in Regional Geography of the Great Plains and Midwest, Physical Geography, and Medical Geography. Dr. Dzik has authored two books, one on Chrysler automobiles of the 1970s and one on the historical geography of a Chicago neighborhood. He is also co-author (with James Piety) of **The Interpretation of Our Physical Landscape: A Workbook**. He has published a number of papers in journals such as *North Dakota Quarterly, South Dakota Journal of Medicine, Geographical Perspectives, Geographia Medica, and Bulletin of the Illinois Geographical Society.*